I Can Make a Difference

# Helping Animals

Vic Parker

Heinemann Library
Chicago, Illinois

**www.capstonepub.com**
Visit our website to find out more information about Heinemann-Raintree books.

**To order:**
☎ Phone 888-454-2279
🖥 Visit www.capstonepub.com
to browse our catalog and order online.

Edited by Daniel Nunn, Rebecca Rissman, and Sian Smith
Designed by Steve Mead
Picture research by Ruth Blair
Production by Eirian Griffiths
Originated by Capstone Global Library Ltd
Printed and bound in China by South China Printing Company Ltd

15 14 13 12 11
10 9 8 7 6 5 4 3 2 1

**Library of Congress Cataloging-in-Publication Data**
Parker, Victoria.
  Helping animals / Victoria Parker.—1st ed.
     p. cm.—(I can make a difference)
  Includes bibliographical references and index.
ISBN 978-1-4329-5943-2 (hb)
ISBN 978-1-4329-5948-7 (pb)
1. Animal rescue—Juvenile literature. 2. Animal welfare—Juvenile literature. I. Title.
  QL83.2.P37 2012
  639.9—dc23                    2011015686

**Acknowledgments**
We would like to thank the following for permission to reproduce photographs: Corbis pp. 7, 9 (© Laurence Mouton/PhotoAlto), 12 (© Rainer Berg/Westend61), 14 (© Wallace, Daniel/ZUMA Press), 18 (© Leland Bobbé), 24 (© Adriane Moll), 26 (© Julie Dermansky), 29 (© Ariel Skelley); FLPA p. 20 (David Burton); iStockphoto pp. 6 (© Sergey Dubrovskiy), 13 (© Galina Horoshman), 22 (© Christophe Péricé), 27 (© Derek Dammann); Photolibrary pp. 4 (david harrigan/Ableimages), 8 (Martin Brent/Britain on View), 16 (SW Productions/Design Pics Inc), 17 (Ulrike Preuss), 21 (Steve Baccon/White), 25 (Christian Arnal/Photononstop); Shutterstock pp. 10 (© Kristina Stasiuliene), 11 (© lenetstan), 19 (© Denis and Yulia Pogostins), 23 (© Kamira).

Cover photograph of children and a dog reproduced with permission of Photolibrary (Pixtal Images).

Every effort has been made to contact copyright holders of any material reproduced in this book. Any omissions will be rectified in subsequent printings if notice is given to the publisher.

**Disclaimer**
All the Internet addresses (URLs) given in this book were valid at the time of going to press. However, due to the dynamic nature of the Internet, some addresses may have changed, or sites may have changed or ceased to exist since publication. While the author and Publishers regret any inconvenience this may cause readers, no responsibility for any such changes can be accepted by either the author or the Publishers.

# Contents

Why Help? .............................................................4

How Can I Help Animals? ...............................6

Encountering Animals .................................8

Becoming an Animal Owner .....................10

Helping Animals in Your Care ...................12

Helping Rescued Animals .........................14

Donating ..................................................16

Help Habitats ...........................................18

Be Kind to Wild Birds ................................20

Endangered Animals ................................22

Thinking Small ..........................................24

Thinking Big ..............................................26

Volunteer Checklist ...................................28

*Glossary* .....................................................*30*

*Find Out More* ............................................*31*

*Index* ..........................................................*32*

Some words are shown in bold, **like this**. You can find out what they mean by looking in the glossary.

# Why Help?

**Volunteering** means spending your time and energy being helpful. Many animals, places, and people need all sorts of help. By helping, we can make the world a better, happier place.

Anyone can volunteer to help, young or old.

Knowing that you have been helpful can make you feel really good.

Volunteering can also give you the chance to:

- meet new friends

- see new places

- learn new skills

- be active and healthy

- have fun!

  **Before you help anyone, always get permission from a parent or guardian.**

# How Can I Help Animals?

There are animals that need help both in your local area and in other parts of the world. Animals everywhere need to be fed and cared for. Some are badly treated or have become **endangered** or even **extinct**.

Butterflies and all sorts of animals need your help to live happily.

You can help animals in all sorts of ways. You can **volunteer** to look after the animals or the **habitats** they live in. You can also raise money so that other people can do these things.

People who try to help wild rhinos need money so that they can do their work.

# Encountering Animals

We come across some animals every day. For example, you might often meet your neighbor walking his dog. Many animals do not like to be touched, so it is always good to ask the owner before you do.

Some animals can be scared easily, especially by strangers.

You might want to visit animals at farms, zoos, or **marine parks**. It would not be helpful to visit a place where animals are poorly treated. So only go to well-run places that also raise money to help animals in the wild.

You can help animals at a zoo by always following the rules on signs.

# Becoming an Animal Owner

Caring for an animal of your own is very rewarding. There are lots of **abandoned** pets that need homes, so you can help by getting one from a rescue center rather than buying one.

If you don't own a pet, you may be able to look after a school pet during the holidays or a friend's pet when they are away.

Sometimes it is more helpful to animals if you *don't* own a pet. For instance, dogs need company and exercise, so it would not be kind to own a dog if your family is usually out all day, or if you don't live near any open spaces.

Think long and hard about the type of pet that would suit you and your family.

# Helping Animals in Your Care

Different types of animal need to be looked after in different ways. You can help your pets by making sure you give them the right sort of shelter and food. It is also important to know how to handle, **groom**, and exercise them properly.

Fish may seem easy to keep as pets, but they can quickly become sick if you don't look after them properly.

Do not feed rabbits iceberg lettuce, as this can upset their stomachs, and never pick them up by their ears.

You can find information in libraries and on the Internet about how to handle and feed pets correctly. You can also join a society for your particular type of pet. Societies can often give you advice on how to look after your pet.

# Helping Rescued Animals

Rescue centers care for animals that have been badly treated, as well as pets that have been **abandoned**. They always need **volunteers** to help feed, **groom**, clean, and exercise the animals.

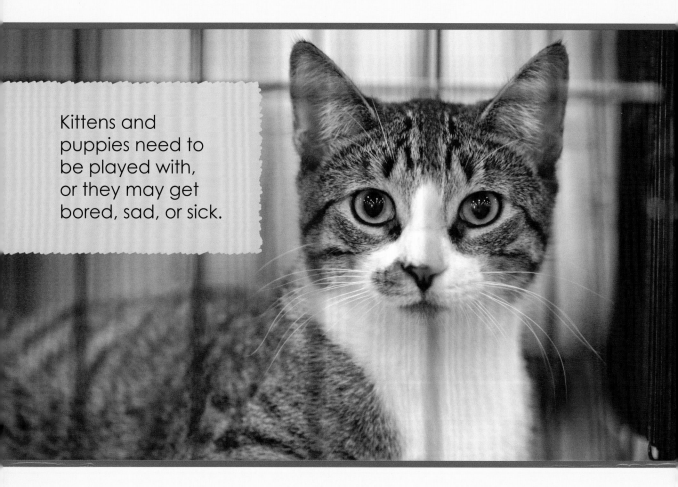

Kittens and puppies need to be played with, or they may get bored, sad, or sick.

You could ask a grown-up to help you bake animal treats, such as dog or cat biscuits, to take along to a rescue center. Here is a simple recipe for some tasty treats.

## Animal Treats

1. Preheat your oven to 300°F (150°C).

2. Put 7 oz. whole wheat flour into a bowl and crumble in one bouillon cube.

3. Add 1 ½ oz. vegetable oil and 7 oz. of hamburger (for dog treats) or fish, such as tuna (for cat treats).

4. Mix with around 10 oz. of water or milk to make a dough.

5. Roll out the dough to about ¼ inch thick, then cut out with different shaped cookie cutters. Bake on a greased cookie sheet for about two hours until crisp.

# Donating

Organizations that help animals, such as rescue centers, always need money to keep going. If you have belongings that you no longer need, you can give these to an animal organization's thrift store to raise money.

Make sure the toys, games, books, and clothes you give are all in good condition.

Giving money or useful items to a **charity** is called **donating**.

You could ask a grown-up to help you sell your unwanted items at a rummage sale. Then you could give or send the money you get to your favorite rescue center or animal organization.

# Help Habitats

To help wild animals, you need to look after the **environments** they live in. For example, picking up litter helps wild creatures who may get stuck in containers, tangled in plastic, cut by glass, or poisoned by leaky batteries.

You could volunteer to join or hold a "clean-up" day near your school or where you live.

Ask if you can have a piece of ground to plant wild flowers and long grass in. This will encourage creatures to visit.

**Volunteer** to make a corner of your yard, or a window box, wildlife friendly. You can make a home for frogs, toads, and insects by loosely piling up stones or logs in a shady corner of your yard.

# Be Kind to Wild Birds

It can be difficult for birds to find food at certain times of the year, such as in the middle of winter. You can help by leaving out leftover breadcrumbs and small seeds every few days.

Make sure you place your bird feeder up high. This will keep the birds safe from cats.

Birds need to wash regularly to keep their feathers in good condition. You can help by putting out a bird bath. Any shallow container will do, such as a dish.

Keep your bird bath topped up with fresh, clean water every day.

# Endangered Animals

Some wild animals, such as humpback whales, tigers, and giant pandas, are in danger of dying out. This is because people are hunting them or destroying their homes. You may want to help stop these animals from disappearing for forever.

Sea turtles are in danger of dying out.

Learn more about **endangered** animals from books in your local library and by looking on the Internet. Then spread the word by making badges, cards, and posters. You could even make up a poem, storybook, or play.

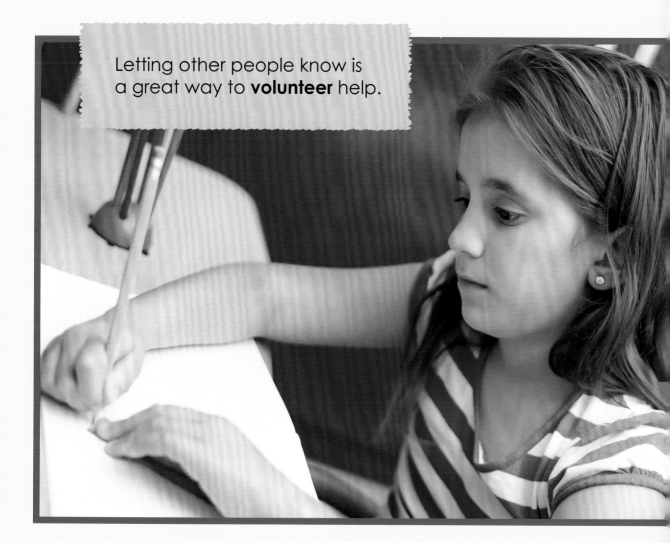

Letting other people know is a great way to **volunteer** help.

# Thinking Small

Often, small things can help animals in big ways. For instance, if a spider is an unwanted visitor in your house, you could stop someone from killing it by **volunteering** to catch it and put it outside.

You can catch a spider in a clean glass or jar and then put it outside.

You could also do little things to fight animal cruelty. For instance, some animals are kept in bad conditions and killed for their fur. Ask a grown-up to check that fur on your family's clothes is artificial, not real.

If lots of people do little things, it can add up to help a lot.

# Thinking Big

You might want to help when there is a big problem. For example, you could help with the cleaning up of animals, birds, and fish hurt in an oil spill at a local beach. If so, see if you can find a team of other **volunteers** to join.

Some jobs can only be done by people who are specially trained. But there are many jobs you can help with.

Asking someone to **sponsor** a zoo or wild animal for you can be a helpful and enjoyable gift.

You can also help with big issues, such as trying to stop animals from dying out, by joining organizations which support these creatures. Perhaps you could ask for membership as a birthday present.

# Volunteer Checklist

To be a good **volunteer**, you need to:

- think of other people, not yourself

- be interested and have lots of energy

- suggest ideas but listen to others, too

- share and take turns, if you are in a team

- keep your promises, so you don't let people down

- be friendly.

Most importantly, *always* check with your parent or guardian before you volunteer to help outside your home. Then they can make sure that you will be safe. They may even want to help, too!

Working with other people you know well can be a safe way to volunteer.

# Glossary

**abandoned**  something unwanted that has been left on its own

**charity**  an organization that helps others

**donate**  to give away something that is of use to someone else

**endangered**  at risk of dying out

**environment**  the world around us

**extinct**  when a creature or plant has completely died out, with none of its kind left on Earth

**groom**  to look after an animal's personal care by doing jobs such as brushing it and cleaning it

**habitat**  area where plants and animals live

**marine park**  area of the sea that has been protected to keep the water creatures that live there safe

**sponsor**  to pay money to help with something, such as the care of an animal

**volunteer**  offer to do something. Someone who offers to do something is called a volunteer.

# Find Out More

## Books

Furstinger, Nancy & Pipe, Sheryl. *Kids Making a Difference for Animals (ASPCA Kids)*. New York: John Wiley & Sons, 2009.

Kaye, Cathryn Berger. *A Kids' Guide to Protecting and Caring for Animals: How to Take Action*. Minneapolis, Minn.: Free Spirit Publishing Inc, 2008.

Olien, Rebecca. *75 Ways to Make a Difference for People, Animals, and the Environment (Kids Care!)* Danbury, Conn.: Ideals Publishing Corporation, 2007.

## Websites

**nationalzoo.si.edu**
Find out all about animals in the wild.

**pleasebekind.com/candotohelp.html**
Explore lots of ideas on how you can care for animals.

**www.kidsplanet.org/factsheets/map.html**
Read fact sheets on endangered animals.

# Index

abandoned animals 10, 14

big ways of helping 26–27
bird baths 21
bird feeders 20
birds 20–21

cats 14, 15

dogs 8, 11, 14, 15
donating 16–17

endangered animals 6, 22–23, 27
environments 18
exercise 11, 12, 14

farms 9
feeding 12, 13, 14, 20
fish 12
fur 25

grooming 12, 14

habitats, looking after 7, 18–19,
   26
handling animals 12, 13

information, finding out 13, 23

litter, picking up 18

marine parks 9
meeting animals 8–9

organizations, joining 13, 27
owning animals 10–13

pets 10–13
poorly treated animals 6, 9, 14,
   25

rabbits 13
raising money 7, 16–17
rescue centers 10, 14–15, 16
rummage sales 17

safety 5, 8, 29
small ways of helping 24–25
spiders 24
sponsoring 27
spreading the word 23

treats 15

volunteering
   checklist 28
   permission to volunteer 5, 29
   what it does for you 5
   what it is 4

wildlife friendly gardening 19

zoos 9, 27